David

Written by Chris Lutrario
Illustrated by Louise Gardner

Collins *Educational*
An imprint of HarperCollins *Publishers*

David was the smallest boy in his class.

He always chose the biggest drum and
banged it louder than anyone else.

He always wanted the biggest bike
and rode it faster than anyone else.

He always took the biggest piece of
paper and painted huge pictures.

He always picked the biggest pencil
and did the most writing.

And David's favourite animal was...

An elephant!